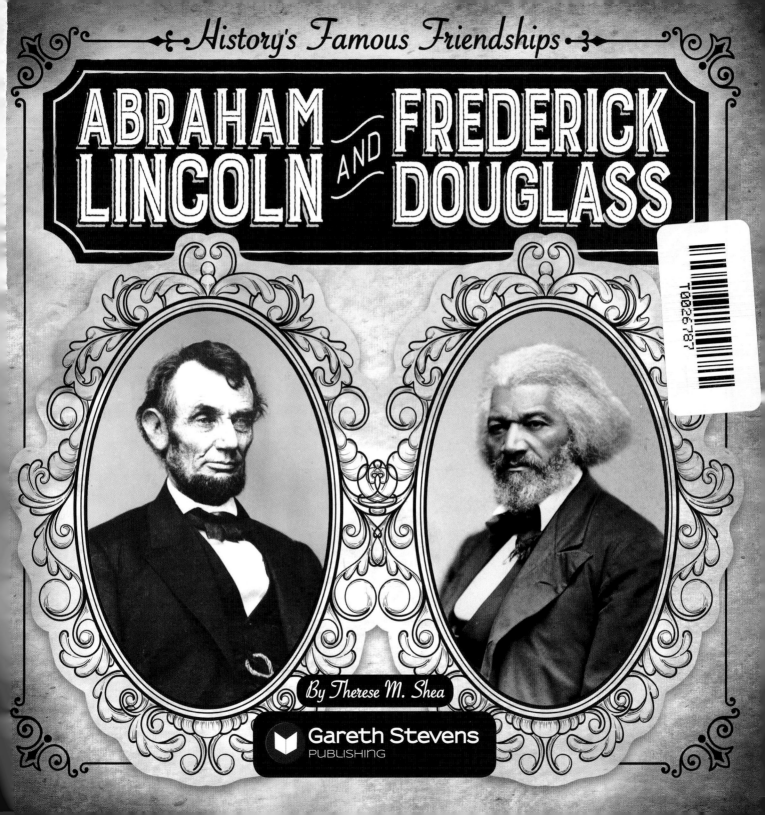

History's Famous Friendships

ABRAHAM LINCOLN *AND* FREDERICK DOUGLASS

By Therese M. Shea

Gareth Stevens
PUBLISHING

Please visit our website, www.garethstevens.com. For a free color catalog of all our high-quality books, call toll free 1-800-542-2595 or fax 1-877-542-2596.

Library of Congress Cataloging-in-Publication Data

Names: Shea, Therese, author.
Title: Abraham Lincoln and Frederick Douglass / Therese M. Shea.
Description: New York : Gareth Stevens Publishing, [2022] | Series: History's famous friendships | Includes index.
Identifiers: LCCN 2020033644 (print) | LCCN 2020033645 (ebook) | ISBN 9781538264874 (library binding) | ISBN 9781538264850 (paperback) | ISBN 9781538264867 (set) | ISBN 9781538264881 (ebook)
Subjects: LCSH: Lincoln, Abraham, 1809-1865--Friends and associates--Juvenile literature. | Douglass, Frederick, 1818-1895--Friends and associates--Juvenile literature. | United States--Politics and government--1861-1865--Juvenile literature. | Social reformers--United States--Biography--Juvenile literature. | Presidents--United States--Biography--Juvenile literature. | Abolitionists--United States--Biography--Juvenile literature.
Classification: LCC E457.2 .S468 2022 (print) | LCC E457.2 (ebook) | DDC 973.7092/2326/.8092--dc23
LC record available at https://lccn.loc.gov/2020033644
LC ebook record available at https://lccn.loc.gov/2020033645

First Edition

Published in 2022 by
Gareth Stevens Publishing
111 East 14th Street, Suite 349
New York, NY 10003

Designer: Katelyn E. Reynolds
Editor: Therese Shea

Photo credits: Cvr, pp. 1 (Lincoln), 5 (Lincoln), 9 (*North Star*), 10, 13, 16, 17, 18, 19, 21, 23, 29 (Douglass) courtesy of the Library of Congress; cvr, pp. 1 (Douglass), 20-21 (Amendments) courtesy of NARA; cvr, pp. 1-32 (background) wawritto/Shutterstock.com; pp. 1-32 (frame) Olesia Misty/Shutterstock.com; cvr, pp. 1-32 (border) Vasya Kobelev/Shutterstock.com; p. 5 (map) Interim Archives/Getty Images; p. 5 (Douglass) The Rubel Collection, Gift of William Rubel, 2001/The Metropolitan Museum of Art; p. 7 Bettmann/Getty Images; p. 9 (book cover) http://docsouth.unc.edu/neh/douglass/douglass.html/Quadell/Wikipedia.org; p. 9 (main) Collection of the Smithsonian National Museum of African American History and Culture, Gift of Joele and Fred Michaud; p. 11 VCG Wilson/Corbis via Getty Images; p. 11 (map) Fred van der Kraaij/ Fpmvdk/Wikipedia.org; pp. 13 (inset), 14 Kean Collection/Getty Images; p. 15 Carol M. Highsmith/Buyenlarge/Getty Images; p. 25 Herbert Orth/The LIFE Images Collection via Getty Images/Getty Images; p. 26 Stock Montage/Getty Images; p. 27 Fine Art Images/Heritage Images/Getty Images; p. 29 (Lincoln) Matthew Brady/Buyenlarge/Getty Images.

Printed in the United States of America

CPSIA compliance information: Batch #CSGS22: For further information contact Gareth Stevens, New York, New York at 1-800-542-2595.

Find us on

CONTENTS

A Time of Trouble 4

Before He Was President 6

Douglass's Daring Life 8

At Odds 10

Praising the Proclamation 12

First Meeting 14

Fighting for Freedom 16

Second Meeting 18

The 13th Amendment 20

Lincoln's Second Inauguration 22

"My Friend Douglass" 24

Lincoln Is Killed 26

Douglass Carries On 28

Glossary 30

For More Information 31

Index 32

Words in the Glossary appear in **bold** type the first time they are used in the text.

A TIME OF TROUBLE

By 1860, the fight over slavery was tearing apart the United States. All Northern states had made slavery illegal. The Southern states believed their **economies** depended on the work of **enslaved** people.

When Abraham Lincoln was elected president in 1860, the South thought he would end slavery. Southern states broke away from the United States to form the Confederate States of America. A **civil war** began in 1861. During this war, Frederick Douglass, a Black man who had once been enslaved, formed a friendship with Abraham Lincoln.

MORE TO KNOW

THE AMERICAN CIVIL WAR BEGAN ON APRIL 12, 1861, IN CHARLESTON, SOUTH CAROLINA. CONFEDERATE FORCES TOOK OVER A U.S. ARMY FORT.

THE UNITED STATES
1860

SCALE OF MILES
0 50 100   200   300   400

Distribution of slave population
(Darkest areas have largest proportion of slaves)

Slave States

Territory, all open to slavery
(Under Compromise of 1850; under decision of Supreme Court, and under Southern claims that slavery should exist until status should be fixed by state constitution.)

Free States

Frederick Douglass and Abraham Lincoln didn't always agree on how to solve the nation's problems. However, they grew to respect and like each other.

Frederick Douglass

Abraham Lincoln

5

BEFORE HE WAS PRESIDENT

Abraham Lincoln was born on a Kentucky farm on February 12, 1809. He grew up poor and worked hard to help his family. He didn't go to school much. However, he taught himself by reading.

Lincoln became a lawyer in 1836. He was also a member of the Illinois state legislature, or lawmaking body. He was elected to the U.S. House of Representatives in 1847. In 1858, he ran for the U.S. Senate. He didn't win. However, he became famous for **debates** before the election.

MORE TO KNOW

IN ONE OF THE DEBATES, LINCOLN SAID, "A HOUSE DIVIDED AGAINST ITSELF CANNOT STAND." HE MEANT THE COUNTRY COULDN'T CONTINUE HAVING SLAVERY IN SOME STATES AND NOT OTHERS.

Many people respected Lincoln after hearing him debate Senator Stephen Douglas in 1858. Lincoln ran for the U.S. presidency in 1860—and won.

DOUGLASS'S DARING LIFE

Frederick Douglass was born around 1818. His last name was Bailey. At first, he was enslaved on a Maryland farm. When he was 8, he was sent to Baltimore to work for a man named Hugh Auld. Auld's wife taught Frederick the alphabet. He taught himself to read and write.

For several years, Frederick was forced to work on farms and in shipyards. In 1838, he escaped to the North. He changed his last name to hide from people hunting for him. He became an abolitionist. That means he worked to abolish, or end, slavery.

MORE TO KNOW

FREDERICK DOUGLASS TRIED TO TEACH OTHER ENSLAVED PEOPLE TO READ. HE WAS WHIPPED FOR DOING THAT.

THE NORTH STAR.

ROCHESTER, N.Y., FRIDAY, JUNE 1, 1848.

NARRATIVE

OF THE

LIFE

OF

FREDERICK DOUGLASS,

AN

AMERICAN SLAVE.

WRITTEN BY HIMSELF.

BOSTON:
PUBLISHED AT THE ANTI-SLAVERY OFFICE,
No. 25 CORNHILL
1845.

Frederick Douglass ran antislavery newspapers, including the *North Star*. He also wrote several autobiographies, or accounts of his life.

9

AT ODDS

At the time of the presidential election of 1860, Frederick Douglass was the most famous African American in the nation. He supported Abraham Lincoln, who was running as a Republican. The Republicans were against the spread of slavery.

In 1862, President Lincoln spoke to Black leaders about sending free Black people to live in Africa or Central America. When Douglass heard about this, he was angry. He wrote that Lincoln was a "representative of American **prejudice**" in his newspaper *Douglass's Monthly*.

In the 1820s, a group sent some freed African Americans to live in Liberia in Africa. Liberia became a country in 1847.

11

PRAISING THE PROCLAMATION

Frederick Douglass thought that President Lincoln acted too slowly. It seemed to him that Lincoln wanted to keep the United States as one country more than he wanted to end slavery. Douglass called slavery a "national sore."

On January 1, 1863, Abraham Lincoln's Emancipation Proclamation went into effect. This statement said that slaves in Confederate territory were emancipated, or free. Douglass praised the proclamation. He knew that Lincoln wouldn't go back on the promise to free the slaves in Southern states. Lincoln called the Emancipation Proclamation his "central act" as president.

MORE TO KNOW

FREDERICK DOUGLASS HELPED RECRUIT BLACK SOLDIERS. HIS SONS, LEWIS AND CHARLES, JOINED THE FIFTY-FOURTH MASSACHUSETTS VOLUNTEER INFANTRY REGIMENT, A FAMOUS UNIT MADE UP OF BLACK SOLDIERS.

Part of the Emancipation Proclamation authorized recruiting, or signing up, Black soldiers for the Northern army.

FIRST MEETING

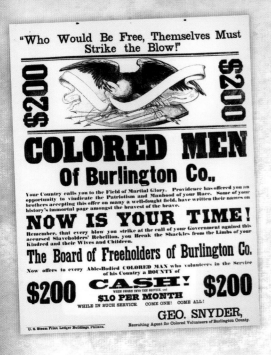

"Who Would Be Free, Themselves Must Strike the Blow!"

$200 $200

COLORED MEN
Of Burlington Co.,

Your Country calls you to the Field of Martial Glory. Providence has offered you an opportunity to vindicate the Patriotism and Manhood of your Race. Some of your brothers accepting this offer on many a well-fought field, have written their names on history's immortal page amongst the bravest of the brave.

NOW IS YOUR TIME!

Remember, that every blow you strike at the call of your Government against this accursed Slaveholders' Rebellion, you Break the Shackles from the Limbs of your Kindred and their Wives and Children.

The Board of Freeholders of Burlington Co.

Now offers to every Able-Bodied COLORED MAN who volunteers in the Service of his Country a BOUNTY of

$200 **CASH!** $200
$10 PER MONTH
WHEN SWORN INTO THE SERVICE, and
WHILE IN SUCH SERVICE   COME ONE! COME ALL!

GEO. SNYDER,
Recruiting Agent for Colored Volunteers of Burlington County.

U. S. Steam Print Ledger Buildings, Phila'a.

Black soldiers in the Union, or Northern, army received less pay than white soldiers. They didn't receive **promotions** as often. They also faced greater danger from the Confederates. If captured, they were enslaved or killed.

Douglass wanted the U.S. government to improve conditions for Black soldiers. He went to Washington, DC, to speak to Lincoln on August 10, 1863. Lincoln welcomed him and listened "to all I had to say," said Douglass. Lincoln promised to raise Black soldiers' pay. He also said he would promote Black soldiers.

MORE TO KNOW

FREDERICK DOUGLASS SAID LINCOLN WAS SOMEONE HE COULD "LOVE, HONOR, AND TRUST" AFTER THE FIRST TIME THEY MET.

After their first meeting in August 1863, Lincoln said Douglass was "one of the most **meritorious** men in America."

15

FIGHTING FOR FREEDOM

By mid-1864, many Northerners wanted the war to end at any cost. To some, that meant not freeing enslaved people. However, more than 100,000 Black soldiers were fighting for the Union. Lincoln knew they were fighting for their freedom and the freedom of all the enslaved.

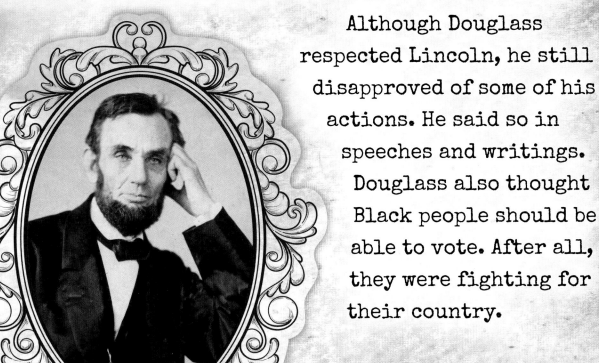

Although Douglass respected Lincoln, he still disapproved of some of his actions. He said so in speeches and writings. Douglass also thought Black people should be able to vote. After all, they were fighting for their country.

Lincoln thought stopping emancipation for all Black people would be a **betrayal** of the Black Union soldiers. He also worried enslaved people might not be freed if he wasn't reelected.

SECOND MEETING

Abraham Lincoln invited Frederick Douglass to the White House in August 1864. Lincoln had a plan. He asked Douglass to organize a group of scouts. The scouts were supposed to go into Confederate states to tell enslaved people to escape to the North. More people could be freed, and the Union would be stronger, Lincoln thought.

Douglass later wrote, "Every slave who escapes from the **rebel** states is a loss to the rebellion and a gain to the loyal cause." Lincoln seemed more against slavery than ever, he noted.

letter from Douglass to Lincoln about the plan for helping enslaved people escape from rebel states

Many enslaved people in the South hadn't heard about the Emancipation Proclamation. Such news would have been hidden from them.

THE 13TH AMENDMENT

Lincoln and Douglass's plan never happened. Later in 1864, the Union army won key battles. The Civil War was coming to an end. As the presidential election approached, Douglass encouraged people to vote for Lincoln.

Lincoln wanted to make sure that the freedom promised to enslaved people in the Emancipation Proclamation wasn't undone. He supported an **amendment** to the Constitution, the highest law in the nation, to abolish slavery in the whole country. The 13th Amendment was ratified, or officially passed, by the states on December 6, 1865.

13th Amendment

MORE TO KNOW

THE EMANCIPATION PROCLAMATION ONLY FREED ENSLAVED PEOPLE IN CONFEDERATE TERRITORIES. SOME BORDER UNION STATES ALLOWED SLAVERY. IT DIDN'T APPLY TO THEM.

The 14th Amendment guaranteed **civil rights** to those born in the United States and those who became citizens. This included newly freed Black Americans. The 15th Amendment guaranteed all citizens' right to vote, although it only applied to male citizens.

14th Amendment

15th Amendment

LINCOLN'S SECOND INAUGURATION

Abraham Lincoln won the presidential election of 1864. On March 4, 1865, Frederick Douglass went to Lincoln's second **inauguration**. He was in the front of the crowd. He heard Lincoln's speech about healing the nation after the war and creating a "just and lasting peace."

After the speech, Douglass wanted to talk to Lincoln. He went to the White House. Two policemen stopped him from going in. They told him that "no persons of my color" could enter, he said.

MORE TO KNOW

THE WAR HADN'T ENDED YET WHEN LINCOLN GAVE HIS SECOND INAUGURATION SPEECH. HOWEVER, THE CONFEDERATE ARMIES WERE RUNNING OUT OF SOLDIERS AND SUPPLIES. MORE THAN 600,000 PEOPLE HAD DIED.

Lincoln had worried he wouldn't be elected again.
The Union successes in the war helped him win.

"MY FRIEND DOUGLASS"

Frederick Douglass saw a friend entering the White House. He asked the friend to tell Lincoln what had happened to him. Finally, Douglass was allowed into the White House.

When Lincoln saw him, he said, "Here comes my friend Douglass." He shook Douglass's hand and asked him his opinion of his speech. Lincoln said, "There is no man whose opinion I value more than yours." Douglass told him he admired the speech. That was the last time the two men saw each other.

MORE TO KNOW

ON APRIL 9, 1865, CONFEDERATE GENERAL ROBERT E. LEE SURRENDERED, OR GAVE UP, HIS ARMY. SOME FIGHTING CONTINUED, BUT MANY CALL THIS THE END OF THE WAR.

the sword, as was said ~~three~~ thousand years ago, so still it must be said "the judgments of the Lord, are true and righteous altogether"

With malice toward none; with charity for all; with firmness in the right, as God gives us to see the right, let us strive on to finish the work we are in; to bind up the nation's wounds; to care for him who shall have borne the battle, and for his widow, and his orphan— to do all which may achieve and cherish a just and a lasting peace, among ourselves, and with all nations

In Lincoln's inauguration speech, he talked about how the nation could heal after the war, "with malice [hatred] toward none, with charity for all."

LINCOLN IS KILLED

On April 14, 1865, Abraham Lincoln went to see a play at Ford's Theater in Washington, DC. An actor named John Wilkes Booth shot him. Lincoln died the next day. At a service remembering the president, Frederick Douglass said, "It was only a few weeks ago that I shook his brave, honest hand, and looked into his gentle eye and heard his kindly voice." He was sad about the president's death. However, he said, "I know that the nation is saved and liberty is established forever."

MORE TO KNOW

MARY TODD LINCOLN, LINCOLN'S WIFE, SENT FREDERICK DOUGLASS THE PRESIDENT'S FAVORITE WALKING STICK. SHE SAID LINCOLN HAD BEEN THINKING OF SENDING DOUGLASS A GIFT BECAUSE OF THEIR FRIENDSHIP.

Douglass said the president's death was a "personal as well as a national *calamity*."

DOUGLASS CARRIES ON

After Lincoln's death, Frederick Douglass continued to speak for and write about rights for Black Americans. He worked for women's rights as well. He held government positions too.

Douglass sometimes talked about Lincoln. He both praised him and pointed out his faults. Lincoln hadn't acted quickly toward freeing enslaved people. However, Douglass realized Lincoln's slow actions had both kept the country together and abolished slavery. Douglass's advice helped Lincoln do both. The bond between Douglass and Lincoln is an important part of U.S. history.

MORE TO KNOW

FREDERICK DOUGLASS DIED FEBRUARY 20, 1895, AT THE AGE OF 77. HE'S STILL SEEN AS A HERO OF HUMAN RIGHTS.

A Douglass and Lincoln Timeline

1809
Abraham Lincoln is born February 12 in Kentucky.

1818
Frederick Douglass is born in Maryland.

1860
Lincoln is elected U.S. president.

1861
The American Civil War begins.

1863
Douglass and Lincoln meet for the first time on August 10. They talk about Black Civil War soldiers.

1864
Douglass and Lincoln meet on August 19. They talk about a plan to free enslaved people in the South.

1865
March 4 - Douglass and Lincoln talk at Lincoln's second inauguration.

1895
Douglass dies February 20.

April 14 - Lincoln is shot.

April 15 - Lincoln dies.

December 6 - The 13th Amendment abolishes slavery.

GLOSSARY

amendment: a change or addition to a constitution

betrayal: going against a promise

calamity: an event that causes great suffering and harm

civil rights: the personal freedoms granted to citizens by law

civil war: a war between two groups within a country

debate: an argument or public discussion. Also, to argue a side in a public discussion.

economy: the money made in an area and how it is made

enslaved: being owned by another person and forced to work without pay

inauguration: a ceremony at the start of a term in public office

meritorious: deserving praise

prejudice: an unfair feeling of dislike for someone or a group because of their race, sex, religion, or another feature

promotion: moving someone to a higher or more important rank or position

rebel: having to do with a person or group who fights to overthrow a government

For More Information

Books

Murphy, Frank. *Frederick Douglass: Voice for Justice, Voice for Freedom*. New York, NY: Random House, 2019.

Murray, Laura K. *Abraham Lincoln*. Mankato, MN: Pebble, 2020.

Susienka, Kristen. *Frederick Douglass*. New York, NY: PowerKids Press, 2020.

Websites

The American Civil War for Kids
www.ducksters.com/history/civil_war.php
Find out more about the events of the Civil War.

Frederick Douglass and Abraham Lincoln
www.whitehousehistory.org/frederick-douglass-and-abraham-lincoln
Read more about this historic friendship.

Publisher's note to educators and parents: Our editors have carefully reviewed these websites to ensure that they are suitable for students. Many websites change frequently, however, and we cannot guarantee that a site's future contents will continue to meet our high standards of quality and educational value. Be advised that students should be closely supervised whenever they access the internet.

INDEX

abolitionists 8

Auld, Hugh 8

autobiographies 9

Booth, John Wilkes 26

Civil War, U.S. 4, 20, 22, 24, 29

Confederate States of America
    4

Constitution, U.S. 20

Douglass's Monthly 10

Douglas, Stephen 7

Emancipation Proclamation
    12, 13, 19, 20

15th Amendment 21

14th Amendment 21

inauguration 22, 25, 29

Lee, Robert E. 24

Lincoln, Mary Todd 27

newspapers 9, 10

North Star 9

slavery 4, 6, 8, 9, 10, 12, 18,
    20, 28, 29

soldiers 12, 13, 14, 16, 17, 22,
    29

13th Amendment 20, 29

Union 14, 16, 17, 18, 20, 23

White House 18, 22, 24

History's Famous Friendships

History's Famous Friendships
ABRAHAM LINCOLN AND FREDERICK DOUGLASS

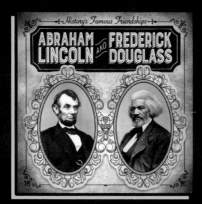

History's Famous Friendships
GEORGE WASHINGTON AND ALEXANDER HAMILTON

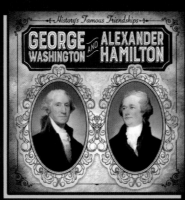

History's Famous Friendships
HELEN KELLER AND ALEXANDER GRAHAM BELL

History's Famous Friendships
JOHN ADAMS AND THOMAS JEFFERSON

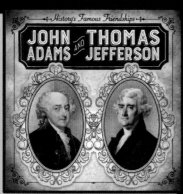

History's Famous Friendships
MARK TWAIN AND NIKOLA TESLA

History's Famous Friendships
SUSAN B. ANTHONY AND ELIZABETH CADY STANTON

Gareth Stevens
PUBLISHING

ISBN: 9781538264850
6-pack ISBN: 9781538264867

9 781538 264850